A Place in Time   Stan St. Clair

A Place in Time

A Place in Time   Stan St. Clair

A Place in Time

A Reconstruction Era novella about the healing of America

By

Stan St. Clair

Historically Illustrated

EDITED BY MICHELE DOUCETTE

A Place in Time   Stan St. Clair

© 2009 by Stan St. Clair,
St. Clair Publications

All rights reserved. No part of this publication may be reproduced or transmitted in any form by any means electronic or mechanical, including telecopy, recording, or any information storage and retrieval system now known or invented, without permission in writing from the publisher, except by a reviewer who wishes to quote brief passages in connection with a review written for inclusion in a magazine, newspaper or broadcast.

ISBN 978-0-9801704-8-1

Printed in the United States of America by
St. Clair Publications
P. O. Box 726
Mc Minnville, TN 37111-0726

Purchase on amazon.com, or at
http://stan.stclair.net

A Place in Time   Stan St. Clair

To Rhonda

A Place in Time   Stan St. Clair

A Place in Time   Stan St. Clair

Contents

Preface
11

Chapter One
13

Chapter Two
29

Chapter Three
43

Chapter Four
51

Chapter Five
64

Chapter Six
71

Chapter Seven
 79

Chapter Eight
85

Chapter Nine
89

Chapter Ten
93

Chapter Eleven
 98

Chapter Twelve
102

Epilogue
111

Bibliography
115

Books for
Further Study
116

Reconstruction Era Quotable Quotes
119

Fictional Characters
120

A Place in Time   Stan St. Clair

Historical Characters
121

**Pictures and Political Cartoons
(Cartoons by Thos. Nast, Harper's Weekly)**

Cover Photo: Richmond VA Crippled Locomotive, Richmond and Petersburg Railroad Depot Created and Published 1865 Source: My Model Railroad, Civil War Photographs Page 5
http://www.mymodelrailroad.net/Civil5.htm

Wesley Enloe – Abraham Lincoln
27

The Assassination of President Lincoln
28

Old Christiansburg Institute
41

Captain Charles S. Schaeffer
42

Thaddeus Stevens Lithograph
50

A Place in Time   Stan St. Clair

King Andy I
62

Hiram Rhodes Revels
63

Tine Works Wonders
69

Southern Justice
70

Visit of the Klu Klux Klan
89

Harpers Weekly Cover
97

Nineteenth century Klansmen
101

The Union as it Was
110

The Civil Rights of 1875
114

A Place in Time   Stan St. Clair

Preface

The turbulent years following the War Between the States in America, not unlike the era in which we live in the early twenty-first century, held enormous challenges for our struggling and divided nation. Race relations were at a pulsating high, war had raised its ugly head, and the economy was in immense disarray. Change and unity were grossly needed.

In this novella of the Reconstruction and healing of our nation, I draw major reverse parallels between the political factions of the eighteen sixties and seventies and those of today.

The main character, Will Patterson, comes from a traumatic past. His mother was reared by wealthy slave-owning parents on a massive plantation. However, she had always rued the life into which she had been born. She thus accepted a simplistic existence as the wife of a humble circuit-riding preacher. Now, he has been killed in the war, and she, as well, has passed away. Will is forced to face life at age eighteen as a struggling farmer in Southwestern Virginia. What chance has he at a meaningful life?

Follow his adventures as he is befriended by an opulent neighbor with a beautiful and charming daughter, is placed in a position of leadership, and catches the eye of the Radical Republican organizers of the Reconstruction. From then on, he is magnetically drawn into the center of their effort, and earns a University degree, effectively becoming the driving force behind shutting down the KKK, and the enforcement of Civil Rights legislations.

Truly, America in the Reconstruction Era was a crucial place in time.

Note:

A Place in Time is a short work of fiction; hence, its main characters are hypothetical. It is based around actual historic events, and real political figures of the day. Any resemblance of the primary characters to other persons, living or dead is purely coincidental. (List at end)

Chapter One

A quadruplet of silvery fingers sprang downward from the boisterous ring of storm clouds encircling the peaked horizon. The angry projections widened, narrowly missing intersection with the caps of the age-old mountains, then slowly dissolved, blending with the grey sea about them.

A momentary clap of thunder was the immediate harbinger of rippling light. What had been but a dampening mist rapidly accelerated to a drenching downpour.

Will Patterson hastened his pace to a jog. Any sanguinity which may have remained from his pleasant dreams of Sally Walker had faded sharply in the inescapable reality of the frustrating scene to which he had just been witness.

She and Hal Bright were at this very moment gliding merrily in her cozy side-porch swing. Now he was being soaked to the very skin by an unsolicited act of God.

A Place in Time   Stan St. Clair

Reaching the front entrance to his tiny cabin, about half a mile around the winding dirt road, past the Walker orchard, young Will made a mad dash for the only place of security which he had come to know for the past few months since his return to the valley.

He had gotten thoroughly peeved with those, whom he had overheard, at what they had obviously assumed to be a safe distance, referring to him as "Wee Willie". Truly, he was but 5'9", but height couldn't determine character. Many of the older folk about had become acquainted with his somber, tall father, God rest his soul, when he had moved there to serve as the circuit-riding preacher for a trio of small Methodist congregations throughout southern Montgomery County, some twenty years prior. At that time in antiquity, Will, the namesake of his proud pa, with only a different middle name, had been but a glimmer of hope in the hearts of his parents.

Before his birth on St. Valentine's Day, 1847, his father had been reappointed to a larger church in Salem. Then the war had carried him away to his untimely demise at the second

A Place in Time   Stan St. Clair

battle of Bull Run on 29 August 1862. Though the enemy had been subdued, his stalwart mentor would be no more by his side.

In states of anger, he had envisioned himself plodding northward, across the Mason-Dixon, in a do-or-die search for the dirty dog who shot his pa. But how would he have distinguished his father's slayer, anyway? Alas, he had been left only with the sad conclusion that he must put the whole sordid mess behind him and move on.

His interest in the tender blossom down the way had aided in his previously feeble attempts to shuck his resentment of being made an orphan before Father Time could mature his views of such abstruse matters. His comforting mother had succumbed to a tossing bout with pneumonia at his enatic grandparents' estate near Roanoke the past winter.

His mother's parents, the Grahams, had been wealthy plantation owners. But now, without their slave laborers, and stripped of their dignity, they were no longer able to tend their fields, and had settled into living out their days in the manse with the weedy fields going to naught around them, and their home in gross need of repair. Their only daughter's death had torn from them, it had seemed, their final will to care.

The cabin and eighty acres, more or less, had been purchased by his father just after wedding Will's darling mother in 1845. The farm followed the course of Falling Branch to the foot of Christiansburg Mountain, and then traced its base to the head of a breathtaking ravine. Here a still, cold spring fed into the branch, and held an open invitation for deer to renew their strength. Will was able to vividly recall a brief visit to this tranquil spot with his father on a hunt. A dainty doe had stood seemingly immobilized at the spring, her breath frozen, and drifting; her captivating image shimmering in the gelid water.

After his father's death, they had moved from Salem to Roanoke, to live with the Grahams. He had been able to receive a basic education, for which he was grateful. He had only the vague memories of that beloved time on the

A Place in Time				Stan St. Clair

farm. The place was now all that remained of his father's labors.

The Grahams, like the Pattersons, were of Scottish descent, and amply proud of their heritage. As a youth, he had sat in awe at the feet of his grandpa Graham, for great durations, learning of their rich history. Both of his grandfathers had been descendants of immigrants who were noble soldiers of the American Revolution.

Six-twenty the following morning found Will rolling over with a grunt to shape a new nest in his familiar feather bed, and escape the blinding stream which poured between the soft calico curtains. The raspy crow of a young bantam cock which had stubbornly roosted in the maple adjacent to his window became a twin reminder that his old Jersey, Bess, awaited his tugging at her swollen teats. She had recently been fresh with calf, which had been sold to Colonel Walker for three much-needed dollars.

In those final moments before arising, Will struggled to remember his interrupted dream.

A Place in Time   Stan St. Clair

His mother had been relating to him one of those familiar tales of her want-free childhood. Her dedicated Baptist mother had hated the ungodly practice of slavery, and demanded fair treatment, if indeed any slavery might have been deemed "fair". Just over two years ago, she had been relieved at Lincoln's great shift of policy by the issuance of the Emancipation Proclamation on New Years Day, 1863, though she was immediately cognizant of its potential aftereffects, particularly upon her husband's inflated ego.

Will's mother-to-be, Mary Lou, had befriended a young slave girl named Emma, in spite of her adamant father's overt displeasure. The two would often be spotted gaily flitting about the fields in springtime, chasing illusive Monarchs, or on their knees at the creek, grabbling for minnows.

Another of his dreams had been both frightening and repetitive. Will had been plagued by it, experiencing night sweats, and abrupt awakenings. While Will and his ma were sojourning with the Grahams, in April, 1865, just nine days after Lee's surrender to Grant at Appomattox, the family had taken a

A Place in Time Stan St. Clair

jaunt to Washington to visit relatives. At the insistence of his great uncle, it was decided that they must catch the comedy "Our American Cousin", a play at the newly-built Ford's Theater, on the evening of the 14th. The house had been packed to capacity. After the play had gotten well underway, it had been suddenly halted, for the president himself had arrived. The orchestra had immediately been compelled to perform "Hail to the Chief".

Later, while at the most comical point, all eyes having been focused upon the stage, a bone-chilling shot rang forth from the balcony. Pandemonium broke out. Screams were reverberating from every section of the theater; the beloved president had been hit at close range.

Only of late had the frequency of the horrendous nightmare reliving this traumatic event begun to diminish.

Will felt an uncanny kinship to the late, great Lincoln, though it had gone unclaimed and unspoken. He had cherished rumors which he had heard since early youth that Abe's true father had been a man named Abraham Enloe.

A Place in Time   Stan St. Clair

His mother, the young and vulnerable Nancy Hanks, the rumors went, had been the ward of Enloe in North Carolina before being taken under the wing of the restless and backward Tom Lincoln. Though Will had no feelings for Enloe, a cousin of his paternal grandmother, the thought of the rumors, heralded as gospel truth by the Enloe family and acquaintances, gave his thoughts of Honest Abe a cheery closeness.

All during Will's chores that morning, his mind kept reverting to Sally Walker. He was keenly aware of the plain truth. He was living in near abject poverty, while Hal was of the bourgeois, and now home on spring break from his first year at Harvard, where he had taken up the study of law.

How he wished that Sally were of a clan less momentous. When he had first laid eyes upon her, a chemical reaction had sent ripples of excitement to every part of his slender body. His thick, ebony hair, well-groomed youthful beard, and undeniable comeliness were certainly in his favor, but his demure personality had kept him from expressing his

A Place in Time   Stan St. Clair

inward feelings to the enchanting object of his affection.

"*Hal is so dadburn transparent*", the thought raced through his mind. "*Why in God's name can't Sally see it? He's just a cotton-pickin' flirt!*".

Colonel Walker had served the Confederacy proudly, aiding Stonewall in the Shenandoah Valley as they held back Mc Donnell's troops in June of '62. Then in November, he had led a brigade in the defeat of General Burnside at Fredericksburg. Yet, it seemed that the colonel was humble in his dealings with life and family. He had been neutral in speaking on slavery, as he was a progressive businessman, operating a general store in Christiansburg, and having vested interest in the bank. His impressive Winesap orchard was tended by his strapping son, six hearty brothers, their families, and those whom they hired, including some former slaves. The war had leveled a great deal of the trees, but the Walkers had labored feverishly to get a new crop going.

The Walkers had but the two children, Tom, aged 19, and Sally, now almost 17. Tom had

A Place in Time   Stan St. Clair

been into apple growing since he was scarce the age of eleven. He seemed a natural to head the business in the future. The store was his pa's baby. The colonel was always up at the break of day, whistling and spit-shining his shoes, dressing to the absolute hilt, saddling his proud steed, and pointing his nose toward the store.

Soon, the morning was half expired. Will had finished his chores and had trekked the three miles to town. The welcome sun was peeking through the dispersing clouds, and Saturday held promises of more pleasant memories than the previous day. As he neared Walker's General Mercantile, the clear tones of the colonel's whistling "Dixie", which met his tender ears, made him to know that his neighbor was in a tolerable mood.

"Ga'day, Colonel. How are you this beautiful morning?"

"Very well, M'boy, and you?"

"Well, sir, I've nothin' to complain about. I need a few supplies to be put on my account."

A Place in Time   Stan St. Clair

"Certainly, M'boy."

And so, the basic needs for the upcoming week were collected, and Will was turning to leave.

"By the way, Son, how'd you like to stop by the house this evenin'? I have a little proposition I'd like to discuss with ya."

Will hesitated only briefly, out of shock. In the last few months, since he had been dwelling around the bend from this family, he had not received such an invitation.

"Why, yes sir", he smiled, "I'd be most honored."

The nearer Will got to the massive white columns of the Walker home, the more certain he became that whoever answered the giant portal before him would be sure to hear the patter of his heart and the knocking of his knees.

He had gently dabbed the coffee spots on the jacket of his only suit of dress clothes, and heated the iron on the kitchen stove enough to

A Place in Time   Stan St. Clair

press most of the wrinkles from the trousers. He hardly needed a jacket on a warm summer's evening anyway.

What in heaven's name could the colonel possibly have to say that would warrant a personal petition to his estate?

"Good evenin' young Massa Will'am," It was the dear mammy who had reared the Walker children. "Massa Walker's expectin' ya. Come on into the pah'la."

Will was quite accustomed to the luxury of fashionable homes. None the less, his heart beat wildly at the curiosity of the visit, as well as his emotional attachment to Sally, whom he reckoned must lurk nearby.

Momentarily, Will sensed a presence just beyond the arch to the dining area, and realized no surprise when Sally's shadow first appeared, followed by her shapely, feminine form. Her long auburn hair was pinned in a delightful up-do. Her lips pursed lightly, and her hazel eyes sparkled like those of a feline as he heard her great him amiably.

A Place in Time
Stan St. Clair

"Good evening, Will. Father asked me to tell you that he will be down in a few minutes. He had a long day at the store, and he and Tom had a few words when he got in. I just don't know what's gotten into that brother of mine. Father simply won't tolerate his attitude!" Sally's speech was prim and proper: undoubtedly due to the tutoring of her mother.

Will smiled. Could she see what he was feeling? He was trying so hard to appear nonchalant.

Sally's words were ended by the precipitate arrival of the charismatic colonel.

"Ah, there you are, M'boy! Won't you join us at the dinnuh table? Miss Flora has prepared another of her fi-i-ine feasts for us this evenin'."

Mammy Flora displayed a simper, and nodded agreeably as the trio entered the elegantly appointed dining room.

Jane Walker smiled gratefully, and resumed her position to the left of the colonel's end chair. Will had never met the beautiful ghost of a lady before. There had been talk that she was sickly, but not being prone to gossip, Will had never inquired as to the nature of her alleged ailments.

Mammy Flora had flooded the lengthy oak table with a boundless expanse of victuals. Will was never so glad that he had not taken time to eat before leaving the cabin. The colonel had not breathed a word about food.

The absence of Tom was nervously obvious, but no one ventured an explanation, or so much spoke of the fact, so Will dared not go there.

During the course of the meal, the Walkers chatted warmly with him on trite subjects which Will was sure had no relevance to the purpose of his presence.

Long before the blackberry cobbler had stretched the lining of his normally flat stomach, his curiosity had gotten much the better of him. He was so torn between being pleasing in his answers to the colonel's questions of his scant existence, and his bleeding heart at being forced into the presence

A Place in Time   Stan St. Clair

of the only female on God's green earth who made him anxious and heated simultaneously, that the evening seemed to wear at a snail's pace.

About the time that Will was certain that the extenuating episode would never end, the laid-back colonel made his long-awaited move. "Come, M'boy, let's adjourn to my study. We must talk."

Wesley Enloe ---- Abraham Lincoln
Wesley, the son of Abraham Enloe,
claimed to be the half brother of Lincoln.

**The Assassination of President Lincoln
Currier and Ives Sketch
Source: Wikipedia article**

CHAPTER TWO

Rambling homeward that evening, in the soft light of the full moon, Will felt like a zombie. High swirling dark clouds threatened to extinguish the moon's glow, but again it emerged unscathed. He thought that surely someone would soon awaken him, and he would realize that the conversation at the Walker estate had been but a figment of his imagination.

He had never considered Tom to be a friend, for the two had barely spoken in the past. But he didn't relish the idea of him as an enemy, either. *One day he will likely show up at the farm and beat the living tarnation out of me*, he thought, *if I take the job. Lord, what am I gonna do?*

It seemed that the colonel had been watching Will from a distance for the past three months. Tom had been, in his words, "a sore disappointment". Will, on the other hand, was "honest, dependable, and the best sort of young man". His brothers and their sons had, as they had put it, "no desire to manage the orchard in the long term". The colonel had asked Will to come to work, immediately, and be the apprentice of his brother, George, the interim manager.

While at the estate, he couldn't help but feel that Walker had an ulterior motive. Was his affection for Sally so darned obvious? "I'll think on it, sir", he had said.

In his dreams that night, Will could smell the distinctive fragrance of apple blossoms flooding about him. Sally was there. She reached for him, her dress loose about her shoulders. Plunging toward his lips, her passion was violent. He grabbed her in his anxious arms, and squeezed her supple form until it seemed to melt into his. Suddenly he shook himself awake; perspiration was heavy on his brow. His body seemed to burn with endless fire, and his heart clanged like a church bell at midnight.

Surely, he thought, *the devil has possessed me.* But what he felt was the normal urge of a man for the woman he loved.

A Place in Time   Stan St. Clair

The decision was actually a no-brainer. He would face Tom when the time came. The chance to be near Sally was a driving factor. Every day at work, he would see her. Though she kept at a distance for the most part, Will could sense that she was not adverse to his presence.

"Hell fire, man, what do you mean?"

Will heard clearly the torrid objections of John Price as he stared into the eyes of the Northerner.

"The South will rise again, you S.O.B.!" John's steaming breath faded into oblivion, but the heat of his words permeated the atmosphere.

"John, that's enough!" Will interjected. "We don't need a fight here. The colonel's counting on me to keep the peace."

"Then you deal with this jerk!"

John was unduly jealous of Will. Since he had been a foreman at the orchard for several months prior to Will's hiring, he had expected some day to be Tom's right-hand man. He might have gotten away with his raucous tirades around George or Tom, but Will would have no part of it. Almost a year had expired. Will was firmly in charge. George was now running a grist mill on his own land.

Will, unlike John, longed for peace and healing of the war-torn South. Though he was yet dubious of the intruding "Yankees", he kept an open mind. To him all people had a good thread in their cloth which just needed pressing out. Reconstruction, as Will saw it, was a badly needed cause of the era.

The stranger stood back for a moment, then stepped toward him.

"You must be the boss around here now, huh?"

"You could say that, I reckon."

John, now out of range, had resumed pruning the trees. It was late February, 1866, before the buds pushed forth their sparkling, unique pink hues.

A Place in Time   Stan St. Clair

"Why'd you come to my defense, young man?"

"I don't stand for anybody being pushed around, even Northerners."

The stranger smiled. "What do you know about what we're doing here?"

"Not a bunch."

"I want you to come to a meeting this Saturday night. Are you married?"

"Ain't hardly. What kind of meetin'?"

"A political rally." His visitor shrugged and tossed his head to one side.

"I don't know. I take it you're a Republican. We're all Democrats here."

"What do you know about Republicans?"

"Not much. Just ain't heard much good."

A Place in Time   Stan St. Clair

"What do you think about getting things rolling again like before the war? And what do you think about giving the Negroes a shot at voting?"

"Never heard o' nothin' like that."

"You said you didn't like to see folks pushed around. Are the colored folk treated right in Virginia?"

Will didn't answer.

"Just come to the meeting. 7:00 o'clock at the courthouse."

Saturday night, out of curiosity, more than anything, Will opened the door to the Montgomery County Courthouse, and gently took a seat. He had heard about the infamous Lewis-McHenry Duel which had taken place just outside that courthouse at dawn on Monday, 9 May 1808. As the story was told, the two men had both gone down, dying in the first rifle duel ever to be held in the state. The event had resulted in the passage the "Barbour Bill" later that year, outlawing dueling in

A Place in Time   Stan St. Clair

Virginia. Will was fascinated by the political process. In a way, he figured that to be the reason that he was attending the gathering.

"The purpose for this meeting, citizens of Montgomery County, and the Great Commonwealth of Virginia, is to look at ways we can get working together to reconstruct the South, and heal our nation after the unfortunate war which pitted brother against brother, and divided so sorely our great nation...."

"Hey, Yankee," came a course voice from the rear of the room, "I hear you fellas are a bunch o' nigger lovers!'

"Yeah!" came another, "whatta ya got ta say about that?" Snickers arose simultaneously around the room.

"Gentlemen, we're not here to start a ruckus. We do believe, like our Constitution says, that 'all men are created equal'. A lot of you around here had slaves, and I know that many of you respected them, and want the best for them and their families."

A Place in Time   Stan St. Clair

Will was just observing, but his mother's feelings of kindness were embedded in his soul.

Mumbles were reverberating from the crowd.

"What's this bull I hear about niggers votin'?"

"We believe that is one way to get unity, and that it is the right of all men."

"I say you carpetbaggers should get your sorry butts out of our state, and go back to Yankeeland."

"Yeah, man, get the heck out of Virginny!"

Will could sit still no longer. "Maybe the votin' thing is a little much for y'all to think about now, but these guys have good hearts. I long for the day when we can all respect one another. Rantin' and ravin's not gonna get us anywhere!"

"Thanks, kid. Anybody else wantta say something in our favor?"

A Place in Time   Stan St. Clair

It was the sheriff who spoke up. "I let these guys come here tonight. I appreciate the young man's comments. I don't cotton ta no colored folks votin', but we do need to be civil."

From then on, the meeting was held without incident. The speakers talked of providing work for ex-slaves to aid in the rebuilding process, resuming good relations between the North and South, and jobs which could be gotten in the North by both blacks and whites.

The featured speaker was Civil War Union Captain, and Baptist minister, Charles S. Schaeffer, who announced that he would soon be opening a primary school in Christiansburg for former slaves.

"The school will be called Christiansburg Industrial Institute. It is being modeled after Booker T. Washington's program at Tuskegee, Alabama. The organization sponsoring it is Friends Freedmen's Association of Philadelphia, run by Quakers. We feel that this area has great potential for good. The students will receive a basic education, and we will be offering studies in trades. Things like blacksmithing, carpentry, and printing for the young men, and we'll offer cooking, sewing, millinery, and the like for the girls. We'll also teach farming and gardening. We need your help and cooperation to make this peaceful."

Only muffled whispers went up around the room.

As Will was leaving, he felt a large hand tap his shoulder from behind. It was the man who had invited him to the meeting. He had been one of the speakers for the evening.

"Samuel Long," the man said. "Just call me Sam. Thanks for coming tonight, and even more for standing up for what is right. What we need is a local partner to aid our efforts. You, as a young person of obvious position at a prominent orchard here, would be just what the doctor ordered."

"I've got my hands full at the Walker farm. I don't think I'm your man. Also, I'm barely nineteen years old." Will furrowed his brow.

"It's your decision, Will."

"How'd ya know my name?"

A Place in Time   Stan St. Clair

"After you stood up for me the other day, I asked around. Everybody knows who you are around these parts."

Will shifted his head from side to side as if looking for the person Sam was *really* talking to. "You gotta be kiddin'! Me? Everybody knows *me*?"

"You're much too modest."

"Hey, if you're gonna be around a while, I guess I'll be seein' ya."

On Monday morning, when Will arrived for work, the colonel sauntered toward him. *Uh-oh,* Will thought, *he's heard about the meetin'.*

"Mornin' M'boy! Word's out that you made quite a splash at th' courthouse Saturday night!"

Will reeled at the thought of what might come next. "Don't reckon it amounted to anything much. I was at a meetin' about helpin' to get things movin' for the South."

"From what I hear it was more than that. You had the nerve ta speak out when that bunch o' hillbillies was achin' ta start a fight!"

Will couldn't believe his ears. "Uh, thank you sir. I was just tryin' to do what was right."

"That you were young man! I'm always findin' new reasons ta be proud o' you! And I heard Captain Charles Schaeffer was there talkin' about the Industrial Institute for Negroes."

Will's expression registered surprise. "How'd you know about that?"

The colonel smiled subtly. "Remember, we were in th' war together."

"Yeah, but…"

"I know what you're thinkin', but there were interactions between officers. I know who Schaeffer is. I respect him."

The pat on the back that followed made Will emit a deep sigh.

A Place in Time   Stan St. Clair

Old Christiansburg Industrial Institute
Schaeffer Memorial Baptist Church
(built 1885)
Photo, Virginia Tech Imagebase

Captain Charles S. Schaeffer
Photo, Virginia Tech Imagebase
A bronze bust of him
has been sculpted.

Chapter Three

A harsh, winter rain was descending by the bucketsful. Temperatures were dropping and the threat of snow was evident. Work at the apple orchard would await a drier and warmer day. A week had flown by.

At just past seven o'clock on that crisp Saturday morning, Will was basking at his fireplace, contemplating his yet untold love for Sally Walker. Hal had not been around for what seemed to him a lengthy spell, though it had been a mere two months. He had remained on amiable terms with her, but now, she had informed him that she would be going away in the fall to attend the University in Roanoke. She had told her father that she would have been just as happy at the Montgomery Female Academy, but he had insisted on the luxury of Hollins University.

His reflection was abruptly disturbed by a sharp pecking at the door.

"Hey, Sam! What in the world brings *you* to my humble abode? Come in, man, come on in!"

"Thanks, Will," he said, taking the door in hand, and moving quickly in from the cold rain. "I'll get straight to the point," he continued, wiping his face with a wrinkled handkerchief. "I've never been one to mince words. I've been writing to Thaddeus Stevens up in Washington. I told him all about you. He's insistent on setting up a meeting. He's got big plans for you, Will."

"Whoa! Hold your horses, now! What kinda plans? I've got somethin' to say about that, ya know."

"Across the South, select individuals are being chosen to join our cause. What's in it for you is the chance for a college education, a way to be recognized, and a future which you could only dream of. You'd have to work to pay for the schooling, of course. We also need your help and cooperation with promotion of the Industrial Institute."

A Place in Time   Stan St. Clair

That night was unusually restless for Will. He would sleep for about an hour, awaken, then toss and turn. This continued until his cocky banty rooster sounded the Sunday morning alarm. Will had been so wrapped up in his work at the Walker orchard that he had rarely taken time to pray in the past few months. He figured it wouldn't hurt to try. "God", he said aloud, as if talking to someone in the room, "It's Sunday... but then you know that. I ain't asked you for much of late, but now I've got a tough one. I don't know what to do. The colonel thinks I was brave at that town meetin'. I've heard o' this Stevens fellow. He's a right important man, I s'pose, in his own way. He wants to see me. Help me know if it's th' right thing to do. Amen."

Suddenly, bright rays of the sun peeped through the grey, and the rain dissipated.

Will's eyes quickly soared through the newspaper article. It was Tuesday, 31 July. A group of blacks had gathered to march, affirming their voting rights at the reconvening of the Louisiana Constitutional Convention in New Orleans. A riot had ensued, in which nearly fifty of them had been killed, and about two hundred more were wounded. Will was enraged. He had been informed of the meeting at Mechanics Institute, which had been called by the Radical Republicans of Louisiana. He felt that the Republicans had made a mistake by reopening the convention, and was more determined than ever to work for equality for both sides. In early May, a similar incident in Memphis has resulted in needless bloodshed, involving Negro Union veterans and police, which had been halted by a detachment of federal troops from nearby Fort Pickering.

"God have mercy on our country!" Will said aloud. But he knew he must have patience. Sometimes his faith was severely tested.

"Dern Scalawag!" The farmer was, pointing in Will's direction, as he rode into Christiansburg early one morning that September. The use of this term, especially regarding him, cut him to the very bone. But he had been convinced that his choice had been guided by providence. The Sunday after Sam's visit in February had been a hinge experience for him. His meeting with Thaddeus Stevens had been more pleasurable than he could have hoped. He had traveled with Sam by buggy for days to the District of Columbia, stopping at hotels in towns along the way. There, a messenger had met them on horseback and ridden along with them to the lavish Stevens' home.

Will had been apprehensive about Colonel Walker's reaction to the trip, and his involvement in the cause of the Reconstruction, since it had been first concocted by President Lincoln, and put into action by Johnson in 1865, soon after the end of the war. But his fears had proven groundless. Walker gave him his blessing, as he had with every new idea which he had presented in regard to the business of the orchard.

Since his return, his efforts were paying huge dividends. As a result of his leadership in local gatherings, many were being convinced that the Reconstruction was a reasonable effort at aiding the South. He was now raising the eyebrows of the powers in Washington.

On 9 April, Congress had passed the Civil Rights Act, giving former slaves citizenship, bringing to fruition the reality which had been intended by the Thirteenth Amendment, in spite of a veto by President Johnson. Though in favor of Southern Reconstruction, this had never been his goal.

Johnson was rather an oddity, Will reasoned. But he could identify with his humble beginnings. Born in Raleigh, North Carolina, he had never attended school. He had become an apprentice to a tailor, and eventually succeeded in his own shop in Greenville, Tennessee. He had married Eliza McCardle, the daughter of a shoemaker, who helped to educate him in the basics of the "three R's". Johnson had developed a flair for public speaking, and entered the political arena in East Tennessee, championing the cause of the small businessmen against the wealthy gentry. His rise had been amazing: becoming mayor, congressman, governor, and senator. He had then been placed, at Lincoln's request, on the ticket under him in '64, in an effort to win Democratic votes for his bid at a second term. Thus, a Southern Unionist Democrat Vice President under a Republican had come to the top office by his death. And Johnson *had* no Vice President. Unrest had steadily grown over keeping him at the helm of the nation. The

Republican Congress was *not* happy. The president had become their worst enemy.

One day at the orchard, Will was again taken unaware by a visit from Sam Long, who was now the head of the Reconstruction effort for both Virginia and Tennessee. He had been occupied with dealing with victims of the newly-formed Ku Klux Klan in Pulaski. What had been formed as a social fraternity by a small group of Southern veterans, to protect their rights against the extremist policies of Tennessee Governor "Parson" William G. Brownlow, had turned violent. Will had thus become his top assistant in Virginia.

"The party in Washington feels the necessity for a native Virginian of your caliber to step into a higher political realm", he said. "Your work with the Institute and the progress which has been made here in Montgomery County has been remarkable. Your name is at the top of the list to be groomed to run for a Congressional seat. It's time for the education that I talked to you about which is offered to those who excel in our cause. They are willing to send you to the University of Virginia over in Charlottesville to obtain a degree in political science. They also want you to study law. We gotta have you, man."

Will was speechless. For someone who had become an outspoken leader, it had been a while since he had been unable to utter a word.

Thaddeus Stevens Lithograph

Chapter Four

Will loved his life in Charlottesville. Though he'd traveled extensively about the countryside, he'd never dreamed of such a fabulous lifestyle. At the onset of the war, the University had been the largest in the South, and only second to Harvard in the nation. Will thanked God that it had been spared by General Custer during his marching though town in March of '65. The troops had camped on the lawn, he was told, but the University had remained operational, and community leaders had convinced him to spare the school itself, which had been founded by Thomas Jefferson. *Maybe he respected that*, Will thought. The only damage done had been to campus pavilions.

Will's time there was passing rapidly. The Radical Republicans had gained control of Congress in the elections of November 1866. The dispute over Johnson's clash with Congress about the Reconstruction, including civil liberties, became more and more bitter, with the Representatives overriding the President's vetoes, leading to the passage of the Military Reconstruction Act in 1867, requiring the southern states to be readmitted to the Union, and conform to the Constitution. Another major dispute arose over Johnson's desire to oust his Secretary of War, Edwin Stanton. This led to a vote by the House of Representatives on 24 February 1868 to impeach the President on the grounds of "high crimes and misdemeanors". The vote to proceed passed 126 to 47.

On 4 March, Will received the following wire:

DEAR WILL STOP A TRIAL WILL COMMENCE IN THE SENATE ON THE MORROW BY WHICH IT IS THE INTENT OF THE CONGRESS TO IMPEACH JOHNSON STOP WILL INFORM YOU OF RESULTS STOP THAD STEVENS

The lengthy proceedings lasted until 26 May, and the various articles were voted on. Following a number of attempts to remove Johnson from office, the impeachment rested upon a single vote: that of Radical Republican, Edmond G. Ross, who finally stood up and pronounced Johnson, "not guilty". The effort

A Place in Time   Stan St. Clair

had failed. Johnson finished his term, returning to Tennessee in 1869.

In August of '68, Will was saddened by the news of the passing of his good friend and political ally, Thaddeus Stevens. Nothing would ever be quite the same.

Several young ladies had shown noticeable interest in Will, and he was sorely tempted to become more involved with one of them. Polly Duke was a lovely, raven-haired, classy local girl, 20 years of age, when he met her. She sat on his right in calculus class. It was the second day of his junior year.

"Excuse me!" Will had reached down to pick up his pencil which had rolled off his desk. At the precise same moment, Polly had leaned forward to grab a book under her desk. Their heads had met, and in looking up, their eyes magically locked.

There was definitely something grand in the person of Polly Duke. As time went by, it became obvious that she was unattached.

A Place in Time   Stan St. Clair

"There's a ball this Friday night at the auditorium," Will said.

"I know."

"Well, are you going?"

"No one's asked me yet."

"I'm asking you now."

"Well, in that case," Polly smiled, "I'm accepting."

The date sparked a warm friendship. Others followed, and at the end of the school year, he finally kissed her.

"I'm going to have to think about where this is leading," Will said. Polly had a light in her deep brown eyes. Perhaps it was the Cherokee of her distant past. Will knew that it could go anywhere he wanted it to.

But Sally still haunted his dreams, though he had not heard from her in over a year.

A Place in Time   Stan St. Clair

The Fifteenth Amendment was ratified in Congress on 3 February 1870, prohibiting any state to prevent a citizen from voting based on race. Will felt a sense of relief, but the law was not accepted well, and would be badly abused.

His graduation in May of that year was the proudest moment of his life to date. How he wished that his parents could have survived to live it with him. But now he could only dream of Sally being there. But she was also graduating from Hollins University in Roanoke that spring. The school was selective, private and expensive, but these attributes had created no hurdle for the colonel in sending her there. She had lived on the gorgeous 425 acre campus, returning home in summers to be with her family. The winter before their graduation, Will had learned that her wisp of a mother had succumbed to a spell of consumption. His heart burned for Sally and her father. His regular letters from the colonel were all that kept him informed of the goings on in Christiansburg nowadays.

"And now we will hear from our Valedictorian, William Graham Patterson".

A Place in Time   Stan St. Clair

"Esteemed president and faculty, fellow students and honorable guests: attending this great University has been one of the most treasured honors of my life. Just to have had the distinct privilege of sitting under the spellbinding teaching of the fantastic professors here has made me a better person. The degree which you have conferred upon me this day will not go unused. I have drunk in the wisdom of many generations which came before me, and have mentally prepared myself for the tasks which life may call upon me to fulfil..."

The ceremony was being held outside, and the breeze puffed gaily through Will's dark hair. After about fifteen minutes, as he closed his speech, a shrill holler caught his attention: a female voice which seemed strikingly familiar was calling his name. Could it be? How could he even muse of such a thing? But it was! *Yes!*

"Hello, M'boy!" the colonel said, grinning from ear to ear.

"Hi, Will. It seems like forever." Sally's voice was soft, yet well-defined.

A Place in Time   Stan St. Clair

Will's heart beat as wildly as it had five years before, when he had watched her comely form emerge from the shadows on his special evening at the Walker estate: the one which had begun the spiral of events which had led to this most auspicious of occasions.

"Hi, Colonel; hello, Sally." Will imagined that the love light surely gleamed in his eyes. He had never seen anyone so sensuous as Sally in this precious moment. Was that admiration on her face? "I didn't dream that you could make it, Sally. I thought you'd be near your own graduation... preparing perhaps?'

"Oh, *Will!* That was last weekend!" There was a shy giggle in her tone. "I so wanted to see you! I'm so proud of what has happened in your life! Papa's told me everything!"

"Sally and I want to take you out this evening, my treat. I spent quite a bit o' time around Charlottesville when I was a young whipper-snapper! But things have changed a bunch since then, I reckon. I'm sure you can show us around."

Attitudes were ripe for change. A number of Northern Virginia families had supported the Union, and even fought for their cause. Will was now able to understand both sides of the issues more unambiguously than ever. He could feel the hurt of the Southerners who had lost their way of life. He could feel the deep pain of the Negroes who had been abused by the system, and longed for equality.

The evening with the Walkers had been most thrilling. But more importantly to Will, Sally had asked if they might stay in touch. Since that night, he had floated on a cloud of rapture.

He had immediately left for Washington, where he was greeted by a delegation from Congress. That evening a black-tie dinner was held in his honor.

"Will, back in '67, as the head of the House Committee of the Judiciary, I conducted a sorta what ya might call an inquiry into creating a federal law department. It'll be headed by an Attorney General. My tries have been thus far unsuccessful. The first time it was presented it didn't pass, but I have every confidence that it shall next time. We were kinda obsessed with the impeachment at first, but now that that issue is out of the way, we're moving ahead. Grant is behind us. We'll need good men around here to help us." William Lawrence was focused on his goals, and could see the young man from Southeastern Virginia was like-minded.

"I've been trying to stay abreast of these things, Sir. They say that your purpose is to insure the enforcement of the Civil Rights Act, and proper implementation of the Fifteenth Amendment."

"Yes sir, young man!" Lawrence exclaimed, "I can see you've been doing your homework. We certainly intend to move with all diligence in that direction. A special task force has been formed by the party to groom you for candidacy as a Congressman from Virginia. If that's not in the cards, there'll be any number of other places for a man of your talents and personality."

"I'm taking it a day at a time, Sir, but I am much beholden to you all for the faith which you have placed in me. I'll do my best not to let you down."

As he opened the letter, Will's heart seemed to skip a beat, or was it two?

Dear Will,

Seeing you was such a great pleasure. You may not have realized it, but Hal Bright married a fine young lady in Cambridge, after their graduation last year. He's not planning on returning to Virginia.

Another thing you may not know is that I have held a torch for you all these years. In college at Roanoke, a young man of substantial upbringing, studying to be a physician, asked me to marry him. I refused, of course, in hopes that one day you might find me attractive. Papa always held such great store in you, and Mama thought you were about the cutest thing she'd ever seen.

I hope that I'm not being too forward. I couldn't say these things before, because I had to see you again, and determine if you might be interested in our communicating. But when we looked into one another's eyes at your graduation, I could see right

A Place in Time   Stan St. Clair

then that what I had felt five years ago was not a mistake. I know that when I asked you if we might write, and when you took my hand in yours upon parting, your heart was warm toward me.

I'll be anxiously awaiting word from you.

Lovingly,
Sally Walker

His answer was prompt and positive.

My dearest Sally,

It seems that I have known you all of my life, and that every moment up to this one has been in preparation for it. With every fiber of my being I am deeply in love with you, and have been so since before we formally met.

As soon as my training here is complete I shall return to Christiansburg.

I am so looking forward to that day.

All my love,
Will

King Andy I
Thomas Nast
Harper's Weekly, 3 November 1866 Page 696

A Place in Time   Stan St. Clair

**Hiram Rhodes Revels
By Matthew Brady or Levin Handy
Library of Congress
Photography Division
From Wikipedia**

Chapter Five

"Will, this is Hiram Rhodes Revels. We're proud to say that our party in Mississippi got this gentleman elected in February to the Senate." It was the voice of Charles Sumner of Massachusetts.

Will denoted the sturdiness of Revels stout body, and gazed deeply into his strong, dark eyes. He knew that change was surely upon them. He had heard of the election of the first African-American to Congress, now he was having the distinct pleasure of actually meeting him. He also knew that the conservative Southern Democrats, of which his family had long been a part, had challenged his election, citing the Dred Scott Decision, because no black was considered a citizen.

"I'm most pleased to meet you, Mr. Revels. I've heard of your heroics during the war. Is it true that you were born in Fayetteville, North Carolina?"

A Place in Time   Stan St. Clair

"Yes. That was my first home. My father was a fine and smart gentleman, part Negro, and part Scottish. He was a free man, thank the Good Lord. I was able to get a good education, studying at the Quaker Seminary in Indiana, and the Knox College in Illinois. I'm so thankful that the Good Lord has brought me here to be a help to our country."

"I see that we have some things in common. My family is Scottish. Though most of them reside in Virginia, and are traditionally Democratic, I also have relatives in Western North Carolina. My father was a minister. And I'm so happy to have been adopted by the Republican Party: the party of Change, with a capital C. Maybe some day we can get Southern Democrats to see the need to unite with our brothers of all races, and fight for a future of equality."

"Yes, sir, but I fear that day will be long coming. There is much hatred and bigotry in our land. As a matter of fact, in '54 I was imprisoned for preaching to Negroes."

"I'm sorry to hear that, Sir. Was that in Mississippi?"

"Believe it or not, it was in Missouri. But let's talk about something more pleasant. I hear that you are hoping to join us in the Congress."

"Perhaps some day," Will said, "if it's God's will."

On 22 June, shortly after Will's meeting Hiram Revels, a new bill was introduced to Congress by Rhode Island Representative Thomas Jenckes, proposing a Department of Justice, and it was passed by both the House and Senate.

A special election was held in Virginia's Fifth Congressional District in November of the same year, as Conservative Congressman Robert Ridgway had died in office in October.

Since Will was being groomed for a run at the first chance on the Republican ticket, he had been asked to go up against Democrat Alexander Rives. However, the Conservative Party nominated well-known Charlottesville attorney, Richard T.W. Duke, a relative of

A Place in Time   Stan St. Clair

Polly, the beautiful young lady whom he had dated while at the University.

"Richard Duke is very well liked in the Fifth District", Will contended. "I wouldn't have a ghost of a chance against the likes of him."

The Republican leaders conceded, and asked him to serve as party head for the Commonwealth of Virginia instead, until a later opportunity might arise. Duke was a shoe in. Will had chosen wisely.

In most 1870 Congressional elections the newly-authorized Negroes rushed to the poles, enforcing the Radical Republican majority.

His duties also included serving as Virginia director for the Reconstruction, and Will was relentlessly on the go. Wanting him to reside in a larger town, they provided an office in Roanoke. Though he was not able to manage the orchard for the colonel, he let nothing dissuade him from finding time for Sally. Each weekend, even through the winter months, he hitched a surrey to his mare, and trotted her down the road to Christiansburg. Their weekends were filled with lengthy talks, and plans for an elaborate nuptial the following spring. The date was set for 17 April 1871.

A Place in Time   Stan St. Clair

**Revels Replaces Jefferson Davis in the Senate
Thomas Nast
Harper's Weekly 9 April 1870**

A Place in Time   Stan St. Clair

COURTESY OF HARVARD COLLEGE LIBRARY

Southern Justice
Thomas Nast
Harper's Weekly 23 March 1867

CHAPTER SIX

"The ordinance of marriage is an institution of God. God saw in the Garden of Eden that it was not good for man to be alone, so he gave him a helpmate..."

Will was pretending to listen, but in reality, he was reminiscing. The six years of longing and anticipating what this moment could be like was finally at an end. Tonight he and his bride would consummate their life-long union.

Sally glanced upward into his deeply warm eyes. At 5'2" she was still seven inches shorter than her handsome husband. She pondered not about the past, but of the splendid future which she knew lay ahead of them. Her hope chest had been stocked to the brim with distinctive china, silver, linens, and knick-knacks. "Peace like a river, love like an ocean, joy like a fountain". The emotions depicted in these stirring hymn lyrics vibrated in the chasm of her soul.

"And now, by the powers vested in me by God, and by the Commonwealth of Virginia, I pronounce you man and wife. What therefore God hath joined together, let no man put asunder. You may kiss the bride."

The colonel wondered when the kiss would end. But what did that matter? He was richly fulfilled in the knowledge that his daughter was in good hands. *If only,* he thought, *I still had my Jane. She would have totally relished this experience.*

The couple had repeated their vows in a spacious white gazebo in the Walker front lawn. Sally's bridesmaid, Betty Jean Smith, wondered what it would be like to kiss those charming whiskers of Will's.

The robin sang sweetly, and the orange of his breast appeared incandescent in the spring sunlight, as he darted from the paw-paw tree on the east side of the Walker mansion. The small tree was now putting forth its rich, red purple blooms. The odor of apple blossoms wafted gaily upon the breeze. Virginia had never seemed so beautiful. What war? Had

A Place in Time   Stan St. Clair

such atrocity really occurred but a few short years ago?

The newlyweds were enthralled in the ecstasy of this place in time. Their honeymoon in colonial Williamsburg was more divine than either of them could have ever imagined. Each evening, the tide dashed in as a rhythmic sonnet against their pale bare feet as they strolled leisurely along the golden beech. The reddish glow in Sally's locks was highlighted in the radiance of the setting sun. Perfection was personified as their love was fulfilled. Heaven most assuredly did exist.

Upon returning to his office, Will found that a telegram had been delivered to the mercantile next door, with explicit instructions to deliver it the minute he returned.

DEAR WILL STOP TODAY AT THE INSISTANCE OF US GRANT CONGRESS PASSED WHAT WILL BE KNOWN AS THE KU KLUX CLAN ACT STOP THIS ESTABLISHED FINES AND JAIL TIME FOR THOSE ATTEMPTING TO DEPRIVE ANY

CITIZEN EQUAL PROTECTION UNDER THE LAWS STOP IT ALSO GIVES THE PRESIDENT THE RIGHT TO SEND TROOPS AND SUSPEND THE RIGHT OF HABIUS CORPUS TO ENSURE CIVIL RIGHTS STOP COME TO ASHEVILLE AT ONCE STOP MEET ME AT THE TRAIN STATION AT NINE HUNDRED HOURS MAY ONE STOP SAM LONG

The honeymoon had ended far too soon, and the Pattersons had been forced to return to the stark reality of the state of the nation.

"As you know, Will, this is our third Enforcement Act to protect the civil rights of the freedmen, and those who befriend them. All hell has broken loose in the Carolinas. I have just met with party leaders. They want to pull in our most efficient and dedicated workers to back us in this. Grant will not hesitate to enforce the law. Just down in Rutherford County, there have been a number of incidents."

"Please go on. What can I do to help?"

A Place in Time   Stan St. Clair

"I'd like to take you down there to talk with a lady this evening. This lady is the sister of a leader in the black community in Boston who has supported our cause. Her husband was badly beaten and left for dead. She is willing to testify to get some justice done. Her husband is hiding out and recuperating with relatives in Raleigh till this is settled. I'm very concerned for her safety."

"Mrs. Jackson, this is Will Patterson. I'm appointing him as a special envoy in this area, for the time being, to help enforce the civil rights of the folk around here."

"Proud to make your acquaintance, Mista Will. Where's you from? I ain't seed you 'round these parts."

"No ma'am. I'm from Virginia. I have some family around Western North Carolina, though. I'm willing to do anything in my power to protect your family, and ensure that the men responsible for this senseless act are brought to trial."

A Place in Time   Stan St. Clair

"Thank ya Mista Will. Ya gonna be stayin' 'round here summers?"

"Yes, ma'am. Sam tells me there's a judge named Logan who'll be in charge of the court.

"Oh. Yessa. He sho will. I done talked wif 'im. An' I got me a good lawyer, too."

Will pushed the curtain back gently. *What the blazes?* His wonder was only momentary. Outside the window, a torch was creeping closer and closer, then, others slowly became visible. A harsh voice spoke at what seemed to be a distance of about 100 feet.

"I know you fellas are in there. Now come on out peaceable like. We got no gripe with y'all"

Will denoted a white-cloth-covered head with roughly cut eye-holes glowing in the dim light.

"We're not coming out," he returned. "Now just back off. We're here as friends of Mrs. Jackson. There's no cause for further violence."

"No way. We want Miz Jackson. Just bring her out and you fellas can leave."

A Place in Time   Stan St. Clair

Sam blew out the lamp, and slowly made his way along the wall to the back door of the small house. The horses upon which they had arrived were loosely tethered at a rail in front, near their unwelcome guests.

Suddenly, the horses began to whinny sharply, and the lawn contained a brilliant illumination. A burning cross revealed a group of about thirty white-robed Klansmen.

"Mrs. Jackson, do you have a gun?" Will said.

"Yessa. Joe kept one in the corner next to the kitchen door. It's got a load in it now."

Will eased to retrieve the musket, and broke the glass in the window nearest the spokesman. A shot rang through the crisp night air, knocking the cross to the ground.

Fire began to spread through the dry grasses. As the Klansmen scattered, Will and Sam grabbed Bessie Jackson by the hand and headed out the back door. A sliver of a moon gave scant light, but the trio managed to

A Place in Time   Stan St. Clair

disappear into the wooded area behind the Jackson home.

CHAPTER SEVEN

"Don't concern yourself, Sally. Everything's fine. My mother always taught me, 'all's well that ends well.' "

But Sally was far from convinced. As his bride, she had accompanied Will on the trip to North Carolina, though she knew she could not remain with him. When he had not returned that evening, she had been frantic. Her love for Will was an unquenchable fire, and she had every intention of staying warm in its presence. Though relieved to know that he was safe, she was visibly shaken when he told her of his somber experience the next morning. She longed for the security of knowing that his body would be close to hers each night for many years to come.

The night in the dense woods was a harrowing adventure, even for Will. From their vantage point, they had watched the Jackson home go up in yellowish flames. On the way out, Bessie had managed to grab a blanket and a quilt which lay on the foot of her bed. The invaders had broken down the door, and upon

A Place in Time   Stan St. Clair

discovering that their prey had escaped, had set the tiny house ablaze.

Their horses had broken free from their relaxed bonds, and briskly galloped away, their tails held high in the air.

Will had walked back to the hotel in nearby Chimney Rock in the cool of the early morning. He explained to Sally that he must spend quite some time there, and held her an extended time of love before she caught the stage for home.

"Sheriff, I'm Will Patterson of Virginia. I'm helping out with enforcing the rights of the freedmen and their families. This is Mrs. Bessie Jackson. I want you to place her in protective custody. We nearly got ourselves killed out at her place."

"O.K., Will. I know Miss Bessie. I know what happened to her husband. I'll see that she's taken good care of. The men accused of beatin' him are here in my jail, so I'll let the Mrs. see after her for now. You stayin' around here?"

A Place in Time   Stan St. Clair

"I'll be at the hotel if you need me."

The trial of the Klansmen started on schedule the following Monday. Judge George Logan, who had been a prime mover and shaker in the local Union League, had been selected as their spokesman at a Republican meeting in Rutherfordton on 5 November 1867.

It turned out that the Klansman had left a message with Joe Jackson that his beating would serve as a warning to Reconstruction organizers that they, not the ex-slaves, were to now be their main target. A family of white locals sympathetic with them had now suffered a home invasion, harassing and beating. This made Will realize that the visitors at the house that night were bluffing, and would have used their fear tactics on Sam and him had they come out at their request.

"These men have been charged with violating the civil rights of one Joe Jackson, a Negro. How do you find in the matter of these six men?"

A Place in Time   Stan St. Clair

"In the matter of John Dixon and Joseph Arnold, we find them guilty, as charged, your honor. In the matter of the other four, we find them not guilty."

"I hereby sentence Mr. Dixon and Mr. Arnold to time served. All of you gentlemen are free to go."

"Mr. President, what a privilege it is to meet you, at last. This is my lovely bride, Sally"

"The pleasure is mine. Nice to meet you as well, Sally. Will, I've been told marvelous things about your dedication to the cause of Reconstruction."

"Sir, when I accepted the invitation of the Republican Party to serve, it was with my whole heart. Regarding anything which is needed, I am gladly at your service, and that of my country."

"It's young men with your zeal and fortitude that we need working with us, Will. It's rather unusual that someone of your background makes such a dedication. But I've been duly informed of your progress. Benjamin Butler has been in constant touch with Sam Long. He tells me that you have served for some time as the head of our party, and of the Reconstruction effort in Virginia, and that you aided in enforcing civil rights in North Carolina."

"Mr. President, I have done only what any other servant of our country would have done in similar circumstances."

"Please, call me Sam. Not to be confused with your buddy, Sam Long, of course." Grant smiled broadly. "That's what my Army cronies called me. My real *first* name is Hiram, Hiram Ulysses. But my mother was a Simpson, and folks thought I was named for her. I became U.S., and a symbol for Uncle Sam. I don't mind, though. I find it quite an honor."

"Okay, Sam."

"The main reason I asked Ben Butler to invite you to the White House is that I have a proposal for you. I want you to work with Attorney General Amos Akerman. He's from Georgia, and you two will hit it off jolly well!

You'll be overseeing the entire Civil Rights Movement in the South. You will now report only to Amos. You'll be under the auspices of the Department of Justice. I feel that this is a fitting position, and does not depend upon the whims of the public, as does election to public office."

Will glanced at Sally. A serene peace shone on her face, but concern for his safety still reigned in her heart.

"Thank you, Sam. It will be an honor to be of such distinguished service. I shall endeavor to never let you down."

Chapter Eight

TO WILLIAM G PATTERSON FOR IMMEDIATE DISTRIBUTION TO ALL OFFICERS WITH THE JUSTICE DEPARTMENT IN THE SOUTH STOP THIS IS TO INFORM THAT YOU ARE TO BEGIN FORTHWITH PROSECUTIONS AGAINST ANY AND ALL VIOLATERS OF THE KU KLUX KLAN ACT WHETHER COMMITTED PRIOR TO OR AFTER PASSAGE OF SAID ACT STOP YOU ARE TO REPORT TO ME IMMEDIATELY ON EACH AND EVERY CASE WHICH ARISES STOP AMOS T AKERMAN ATTORNEY GENERAL

Will breathed in deeply, and then slowly exhaled, his jaws puffed. It was July 1871. He knew that the job at hand was not an easy task. Though the incidents in North Carolina, and some in Mississippi, had already warranted trials, South Carolina was now at the forefront of the violations, and was out of control. Even greater than his dread of the assignment was his leaving again, and without Sally.

A Place in Time   Stan St. Clair

At the close of the war, the railroads in the South had been greatly destroyed, and were now only beginning to be rebuilt.

It was with much sorrow that he packed his bags, kissed his wife goodbye, and boarded the stage coach in Roanoke, heading south. There were three stops before changing coaches in Asheville, and beginning the final leg of the trip to Spartanburg.

Wednesday 18 October 1871
Spartanburg, SC

My Dearest Sally,

The time away from you is such pain. I must inform you of the latest developments. I pray that this will lead to completion of this phase of my mission. Last Thursday the President issued a proclamation ordering Klansmen here to disperse and surrender all of their weapons. Of course, they ignored his order. Yesterday, he suspended habeas corpus, and sent in federal troops to help the marshal make the needed arrests. They are beginning, but will, I'm sure, take quite a while to complete.

A Place in Time   Stan St. Clair

I shall miss you dearly, as I have each day I have been away. I shall, as always, stay in touch.

All my love,
Will

Thursday 26 October 1871
Home

My Dear Husband,

I am glad to hear that Sam Grant has finally taken charge, and is making good on the law which he enacted regarding this grave and unfortunate situation in which our beloved South finds itself.

I had hoped to tell you this to your face, as it is is not something to learn by means of letter. I am to become the mother of our child in about five months.

Father has been so generous as to allow Mammy Flora to stay with me for the past several weeks, as he is concerned that I not be alone in my present condition. I am anxiously awaiting your return. Please come as soon as it is feasible. Mammy Flora is now in her sixty-forth year, and more importantly, I need your strength to keep on going.

Love forever,
Sally

By year's end, hundreds of arrests had been made, many Klansmen had left the country, and over five hundred had turned themselves in. Some who gave dispositions were released There were so many involved that the legal systems in these counties were unable to handle them. Only serious offenders were prosecuted. Though arrests continued the following year, most was settled there by the end of 1871.

After the letter from Sally, Will was granted permission to return to Roanoke.

A Place in Time   Stan St. Clair

CHAPTER NINE

"I am so glad that this scene is not so common any more" Will was staring at the drawing on page 160 of Harper's Weekly. It was February 1872.

VISIT OF THE KU KLUX KLAN

The scene depicted was similar to many incidents which had occurred across the South. The artist had depicted a peaceable Negro couple in their tiny cabin, fearing nothing, when suddenly the door is forced open by a Klansman with gun in hand to take the life of the old gentleman sitting by the fireplace whose only crime is the fact that he is not white.

"I need to give credit, he told Sally, to those who have helped us to bring this violence to a close. Our nation is almost free from this curse."

28 February 1872
Roanoke, Virginia

Dear Amos,

It is with great pride and a thankful heart that I write to you today. I respectfully request the authority hold meetings in town halls around the country, primarily in the states of Georgia, North and South Carolina, Louisiana, Mississippi, Alabama, and Tennessee, where our problems were so severe. People need to be thanked for their cooperation, and be educated in the complete removal of bigotry which still threatens our future as united states in which we can all be treated as equals.. The final victory is within our grasp.

A Place in Time   Stan St. Clair

My wife is due to give birth to our child in the spring, and after this event, I humbly ask your permission to begin such a campaign.

Sincerely,

Your thankful servant,

William G. Patterson

15 March 1872
Washington, DC

Dear Will,

It is with my greatest respect that I grant your request for the authority to hold a successive series of town meetings in the states which you mentioned. Funds previously allocated for Reconstruction projects will be made available as needed Please find enclosed a bank note for $50 with which to begin your campaign for said meetings. I am sending letters to all state leaders urging them to cooperate to the fullest extent in making this a most successful campaign. Your compliance to my previous communication to enforce the laws in this matter has yielded great rewards.

I offer my congratulations to you and Sally on the impending addition to your family.

Please keep me apprised as to when you begin your most worthy effort, and the results as they occur.

Respectfully Yours,

Amos T. Akerman

Chapter Ten

"It's a boy!" the midwife exclaimed, excitedly, as she began the cautious cleaning of the new pink arrival.

"That's wonderful!" Will said with great ecstasy. But a slight smile was all that Sally could manage, as she laid her head back on the pillow.

It was Monday, 15 April 1872. Sally had insisted on being home with her father, and Mammy Flora was close at her side. The cycle of time had once again brought the colorful and aromatic blossoms to their sublime height, and nature beckoned even the most timid visitor to roam admiringly about the Walker estate.

Will felt a special pleasure in their return, even for the brief interlude that it must be. He was pleased to be of service to the country, while he could never deny the magnetism which he felt to his roots. Not yet having concluded his twenty-eighth year, he already had enjoyed more satisfaction in living that most men with more many years under their belts.

"Have you decided on a name," the midwife asked.

"We've agreed to call him William, after his father, he'll by William Graham Patterson II," Sally managed. "Had we birthed a girl, her name would have been Jane, after my mother."

"Here, Sally, hold your son."

"Thank you." Her voice was gaining strength, but her countenance was still ashen.

"My, but he's a darlin' of a child, Miss Sally," Mammy Flora said, shaking her head slowly from side to side. "I ain't never seed nothin' any prettier, no ma'am, I ain't!"

"Thanks, Flora," Will said. "We appreciate all you've done for us. You won't go unrewarded."

"Mammy Flora is the best," the colonel said, with deep sincerity in his voice. "I don't know what we'd ever have done without her all

A Place in Time   Stan St. Clair

these years. The Lord has a special place for her, I just know he has. God bless ya, Mammy!"

"Aw, pshaw! T'was nothin', Massa, I loved ever' moment of it. An' I'll be here as long as ya'll don't kick me out!"

"Are you kiddin'? Kick you out? You're just like a member of our family. You're not goin' anywhere! An' I ain't your master!"

"Yessa, I knows. Jes' don't seem proper not callin' ya that. Hey, y'all know I got th' dinner waitin'. You're favorite, Miss Sally! Chicken an' dumplin's wif all the extrys! Green beans, mashed tatters, cole slaw, an' biscuits an' gravy!"

Sally groaned. "I can't eat all that stuff now! Just bring me a bit of potatoes and gravy, and a glass of milk. I'm sure Papa and Will can get away with a bunch of it. Maybe you can save some for later. Put it in the ice box."

"Sho, Miss Sally, sho nuff!"

A Place in Time   Stan St. Clair

"So long, Papa. We'll see you before long. At least Roanoke is but a short buggy ride from here."

"See you soon pumpkin! Take care of my little man for me. I'll likely be down before you can say 'Jack Robinson' Ya can't keep a grandpa away from his little one, ya know."

Billy would be two weeks old in two days. Will thought that going home on a Saturday would be best. They would have the balance of the weekend to be a family before Monday rang the bell of reality in his head.

Due to spring rains, Falling Branch was up slightly at the ford, and Will had to crack the whip just a bit for his mare. The water came up on the surrey wheels to just under the hubs, but the gentle horse gave no more objections, and they were soon on their way.

Low-lying clouds swirled merrily in the heavens above, but sunshine dominated their journey. Within two hours, they were home. Though much was the same, everything now seemed different.

A Place in Time   Stan St. Clair

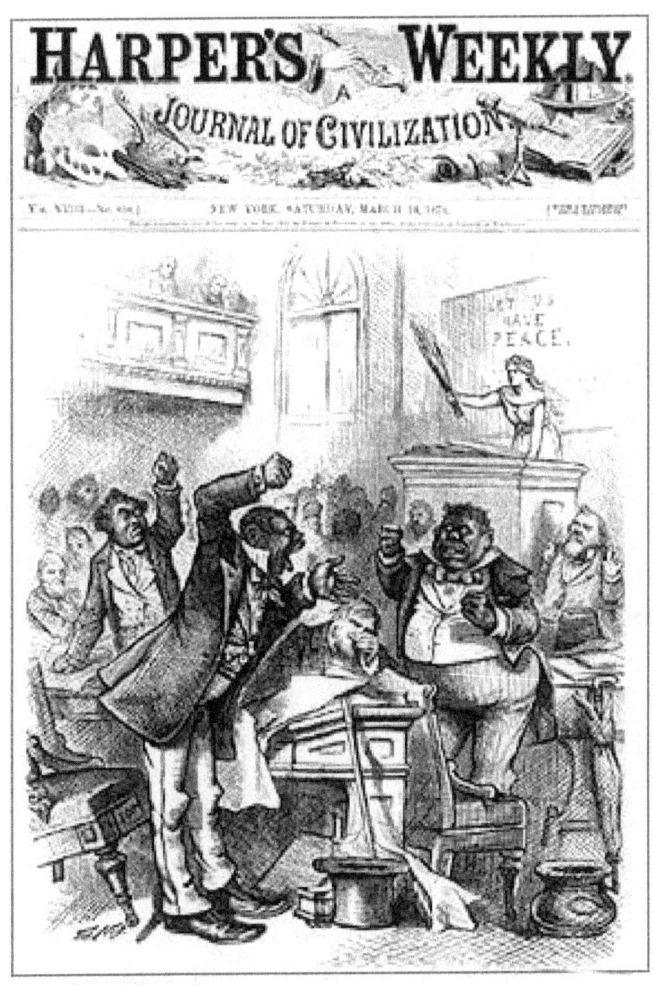

Harper's Weekly Cover 14 March 1874
Showing black legislators
Thomas Nast

CHAPTER ELEVEN

"Doctor, I'm Sally Patterson. I received word by wire that my husband was in this hospital."

"William Patterson?"

"Yes. Can you please tell me exactly what happened, and how he is fairing? May I see him? Is he going to be alright?"

"One question at a time, please ma'am. First, I must tell you that your husband has been the victim of a severe beating. He was found lying face down in a ditch out on Long Hollow Road about midnight of the night before last. A passer-by, who was afoot, heard a groaning and went over to find him. He was near a farm house, and the gent who lived there helped load him on his wagon and brought him in. Your husband, being well-dressed, I assumed that someone had a vendetta against him. But I didn't realize the problem until I found his wallet with papers identifying him. I had read a handbill which had been passed out in Nashville a few days back stating that he would be holding a town meeting at the courthouse that night in regard to racial equality. Then I remembered hearing about a small group from Pulaski who was coming to protest the shutting down of the Klan, and try to stop the meeting. There aren't many left around here who would have dared to back them."

"Lord, have mercy! And how is he now?"

"He's resting as well as can be expected. I administered a dose of morphine about thirty minutes ago. When he starts to come to, he'll be in a considerable amount of pain. And he doesn't look too good either. His face is cut and swollen, and his eyes are blackened. Just thought you should be aware, ma'am."

"May I go in and see him?"

"He won't realize that you're there for a spell. But I'm going to let you go on in. Just sit by his bed till he comes to. I'm sure he'll be happy to know you're here. He's in room number ten. Back down the hall on the right. The number's on the door."

Will had previously organized a police force which had taken action in Arkansas and Tennessee. After the assemblies which he had held in major cities throughout the southern states, the movement had been almost fully dissolved. The meeting in Nashville, to have been his last, at which he gave praise for the good progress which had been made, had been held Saturday evening, 15 June 1872. The dissenters had slipped in near the conclusion, following Will to his hotel. After he had gone inside, a knock came at his door, claiming to be the housekeeper making sure he had everything he required. Two burley men, both over six feet tall, jumped in, one wielding a pistol, the other gagging him. He was then slipped out a side door, and taken to the country road where he was beaten and left to die.

"O-h-h-h, where am I?" Will rubbed his beard gently, seemingly cognizant of the cuts within it.

"I'm here, Darling. I'm right here. Everything's going to be alright, now. When you are able to travel, I'm taking you home."

Within five days Will was enough improved to leave. The men responsible were located from tips given by locals, and brought to justice. The dreaded Klan was effectively out of operation for that era.

Nineteenth century Klansmen

Chapter Twelve

HOLLY SPRINGS, MISS., November 6, 1875.

TO HIS EXCELLENCY, U. S. GRANT, President of the United States:

. . . Since reconstruction, the masses of my people have been, as it were, enslaved in mind by unprincipled adventurers, who, caring nothing for country, were willing to stoop to anything no matter how infamous, to secure power to themselves, and perpetuate it. My people are naturally Republicans, and always will be, but as they grow older in freedom so do they in wisdom. A great portion of them have learned that they were being used as mere tools, and, as in the late election, not being able to correct existing evils among themselves, they determined by casting their ballots against these unprincipled adventurers, to overthrow them.

My people have been told by these schemers, when men have been placed on the ticket who were notoriously corrupt and dishonest, that they must vote for them; that the salvation of the party depended upon it; that the man who scratched a ticket was not a Republican. This is only one of the many means these unprincipled demagogues have devised to perpetuate the intellectual bondage of my people. To defeat this policy, at the late election men, irrespective of race, color, or party affiliation, united, and voted together against men known to be incompetent and dishonest. I cannot recognize, nor do the mass of my people who read, recognize the majority of the officials who have been in power for the past two years as Republicans. . . .*

The great mass of the white people have abandoned their hostility to the general government and Republican principles, and to-day accept as a fact that all men are born free and equal, and I believe are ready to guarantee to my people every right and privilege guaranteed to an American citizen. The bitterness and hate created by the late civil strife has, in my opinion, been obliterated in this state, except perhaps in some localities, and would have long since been entirely obliterated, were it not for some unprincipled men who would keep alive the bitterness of the past, and inculcate a hatred between the races, in order that they may aggrandize themselves by office, and its emoluments, to control my people, the effect of which is to degrade them. As an evidence that party lines in this state have been obliterated, men were supported without regard to their party affiliations, their birth, or their color, by those who heretofore have acted with the Democratic party, by this course giving an evidence of their sincerity that they have abandoned the political issues of the past, and were only desirous of inaugurating an honest state government, and restoring a mutual confidence between the races. I give you my opinion, that had our state adhered to Republican principles, and stood by the platform upon which it was elected, the state to-day would have been upon the highway of prosperity. Peace would have prevailed within her borders, and the Republican party would have embraced within her folds thousands of the best and purest citizens of which Mississippi can boast, and the election just passed would have been a Republican victory of not less than eighty to a hundred thousand majority; but the dishonest course which has been pursued has forced into silence and retirement nearly all of the leading Republicans who organized, and have heretofore led the party to victory. A few who have been bold enough to stand by Republican principle, and condemn dishonesty, corruption, and incompetency have been supported and elected by overwhelming majorities. If the state administration had adhered to Republican principles, advanced patriotic measures, appointed only honest and competent men to office, and sought to restore confidence between the races, bloodshed would have been

A Place in Time   Stan St. Clair

unknown, peace would have prevailed, Federal interference been unthought of; harmony, friendship, and mutual confidence would have taken the place of the bayonet....

H. R. REVELS.

The letter had been written four days after the election of Governor Ames in Mississippi. Fights were now almost as common between factions of the Republican Party as they were between them and the Democrats.

Will was saddened at the division. He greatly admired Hiram Revels, and he shared his desire for equality of all, and not one-sided manipulation, greed and selfishness. He would fight more fiercely than ever to see it accomplished,

A tiny tear formed in Billy's eye as he gazed wide-eyed at the stones. His father had told him of the brave death of his grandfather, and the passing of his faithful and loving grandmother not long thereafter.

Billy was now five. He had begged his father to be taken to the Patterson Family Graveyard.

A Place in Time					Stan St. Clair

He had been told that they were both now in Heaven with Jesus. "When can I go see them?" had been his innocent response.

"Well, Billy, we can't go see them till our life here on earth is over. But their bodies are buried near Christiansburg. "

"Well, Pa, let's go there. Please? OK?"

"The next time we go visit Grandpa Walker, Ma and I will take you there. But it's just a lonely spot above the church house on the hill."

"OK, Pa, but I wanta go anyway."

It was summer of '77. Though his duties were much less strenuous than during the reign of the Klan, Will was serving under the fourth Attorney General, Alfonzo Taft of Ohio. After the letter of Revels to Grant, Will had become a national advocate of equality for all, and had regularly corresponded with Revels during his presidency of Shaw College, and beyond.

Rutherford B. Hayes's election in '76 had been hotly disputed. The Republican control was in grave danger. Having lost the popular vote to Democratic candidate Samuel Tilden, he was elected by a single electoral vote. A temporary body, known as the Electoral Commission had been created by Congress consisting of fifteen members, to decide the issue. These members consisted of five representatives, five senators, and five Supreme Court Justices. Eight were Republicans, seven Democrats. The Republican majority had been all that saved the election of Hayes. The decision had been rendered months after the election, and had become known as the Compromise of 1877.

The old family cemetery was in bad need of upkeep, so Will contacted a former school friend who had stayed in the area between Christiansburg and Blacksburg. Will was delighted when he gladly agreed to become the regular caretaker.

Will was proud to have been chosen for the special tasks to which he had been assigned. The Reconstruction, even with all of its problems, had changed the landscape of America forever. Though he never was to serve in the Congress, the South again would rise

A Place in Time   Stan St. Clair

above the ashes of despair. Negroes were able to work without fearing for their lives, and have homes of their own.

Special Field Orders, number fifteen, issued by General Sherman immediately after the war, granting former slaves "forty acres and a mule", though fueling the rise to such gross hatred as the formation of the Ku Klux Klan, had also served the purpose for which it was intended: it had given hope to those who had none. Now that the Klan had been out of operation for these past five years, hope was growing in the hearts of the former slaves.

Sally looked into her husband's eyes. She had never regretted her decision to be a stay-at-home mother. She could see both pride and hurt, but she knew that the hurt was softening in the new world which was beginning to emerge. The battle would still be long. Many continued to view blacks as second class citizens for over one hundred years.

"Some day," Will said, "some day I pray that our grandchildren and great grandchildren will look back on our day and see the progress which has been made. But I also pray that our

A Place in Time   Stan St. Clair

descendents will not be content until all Americans have equal rights; until all can vote honorably, and all can stand proud and say, 'I am an American, a citizen of the greatest nation in the world.'"

**The Union as it Was
Thomas Nast
Harper's Weekly
24 October 1874**

EPILOGUE

Will Patterson lived to the age of eighty-three, and saw his grandchildren, great-grandchildren and even a great-great granddaughter.

After the presidency of Hayes was ended in early 1881, even though Garfield was elected, the Democrats were gaining more control in Congress. Will retired from politics, and opened a successful general store in Christiansburg, where he was to live out the remainder of his days in peace.

In 1895, Booker T. Washington took over the leadership of Christiansburg Technical Institute, and the school grew rapidly, serving Southwestern Virginia for over one hundred years.

On his eightieth birthday, February 14, 1927, he was honored at a banquet held at the City Hall in Roanoke. Over three hundred were in attendance, comprised of both blacks and whites, many the descendents of the former slaves whom he served, and the party members of his generation.

He and Sally had brought a daughter into the world in 1874, at Billy's age seven. Her name was Jane, and she had become the wife of a prominent banker in Richmond. Billy and Jane never forgot the love which had been so richly given by their parents. Billy, with the support of his wife, Sara, became a minister in the Presbyterian Church. His first born son continued the tradition of carrying on the name of his grandfather.

Three of their grandsons had served with honor in the Great World War, and one in the Mexican American War. The Patterson family had scattered about the country, from Maryland to South Carolina.

On 22 May in the year of our Lord, 1930, Will Patterson, with his beloved Sally, Billy and Jane at his side, peacefully passed from this life to the next.

Hal Bright was divorced in the wake of an affair, and was eventually shot in a barroom brawl in an argument over a woman.

A Place in Time   Stan St. Clair

Today, we have undergone many battles in the effort to achieve Civil Rights for all. In the mid twentieth century, Dr. Martin Luther King championed a cause which has mushroomed since his death. In spite of tough conditions, and a split nation, on 20 January 2009, Barack Obama became then first black president of these United States. Like Hiram Revels, he made history which seemed at the time unlikely.

It was the "Radical" Republican Party who elected Revels, a quite different group from the Conservative Republicans of today. Obama arrived on the wings of Democratic Party cries for change. The Democrats have now come full circle in the cause of Civil Rights. Over time, one thing that will never fail is the fact of change. It is my prayer and hope that proper changes will again unite our nation, that political parties will put aside their differences, and that we will, as never before, become, "One Nation, Under God."

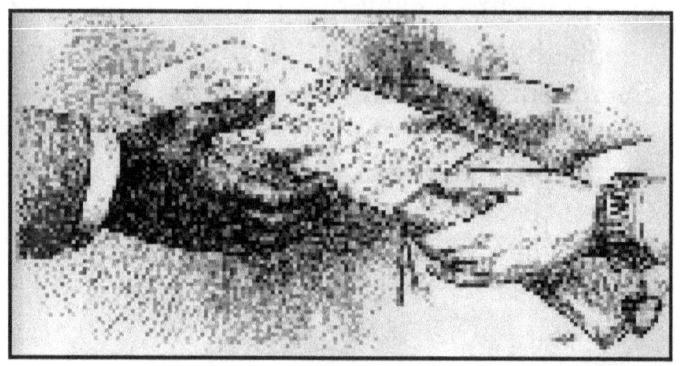

The Civil Rights Act of 1875
Thomas Nast
Source: The Cartoons of Thomas Nast

BIBLIOGRAPHY

Christiansburg, Montgomery County, Virginia, In the Heart of the Alleghenies
Lula Porterfield Givens
Edmonds Printing, Inc. Pulaski, VA 1981
Pp 49-52 (Lewis- McHenry Duel)
Montgomery Female College (pp 71-74)

Reconstruction in Mississippi
James Willard Garner
Macmillan 1091, pp 399,400
(Letter of Hiram R. Revels to President U.S. Grant)

Harpers Weekly Editions during Reconstruction Era 1965-1875 (Cartoons of Thomas Nast)

A number of free Internet articles were also utilized for accuracy of historical events.

BOOKS FOR FURTHER STUDY
In order of Publication:
Oldest to newest

The Invisible Empire:
The Story of the Ku Klux Klan
©1939 Stanley F. Horn
Houghton Mifflin Company, Boston, MA

The Era of Reconstruction 1865-1877 [2 vols.]
©1965 Kenneth M. Stamp , Vintage Books,
Random House of Canada, Ltd. Toronto, ON

Carpetbagger's Crusade:
The Life of Albion Winnegar Tourgee
©1965 Otto H. Olsen
The Johns Hopkins University Press,
Baltimore, MD

The Freedman's Bureau in South Carolina
1865-1872
©1967 Martin Abbott
University of North Carolina Press,
Chapel Hill, NC

A Place in Time   Stan St. Clair

The Fiery Cross:
The Ku Klux Klan in America
© 1987 Wyn Craig Wade
Simon and Shuster, NY, NY

The Work of Reconstruction:
From Slave to Wage Laborer
In South Carolina
© 1994 Julie Saville
Cambridge University Press,
Cambridge, MA

The Day Dixie Died
Southern Occupation 1865-1866
©2001 Thomas and Deborah Goodrich
Stackpole Books, Mechanicsburg, PA

Reconstruction Era Biographies
(Ulysses S. Grant, Rutherford B. Hayes,
Edwin M. Stanton, others)
©2004 Roger Matuz, Lawrence W. Baker,
Editors, Thomson Gale Research Florence, KY

Reconstruction Era Almanac
©2004 Kelly King Howes, Lawrence W. Baker,
Editors, Thomson Gale Research Florence, KY

A Place in Time   Stan St. Clair

The Encyclopedia of the Reconstruction Era
©2006 Richard Zuczek and Eric Fonder
Greenwood Publishing Group, Westport, CT

The Reconstruction Era
©2006 Betty Stroud and Virginia Schomp
Marshall Cavendish, Inc.,
Tarrytown, NY

West from Appomattox:
The Reconstruction of America after the Civil War
©2007 Heather Cox Richardson
Yale University Press, New Haven, CT

The Reconstruction Era, Primary Documents From 1865 to 1877
©2008 Donna L. Dickerson
Greenwood Publishing Group, Westport, CT

A Place in Time   Stan St. Clair

Reconstruction Era Quotable Quotes

Strip the proud nobility of their bloated estates, reduce them to a level with plain republicans, send forth to labor, and teach their children to enter the workshops or handle the plow, and you will thus humble proud traitors.

Thaddeus Stevens

Nations, like individuals, are punished for their transgressions.

Ulysses S. Grant.

The President of the United States of necessity owes his election to office to the suffrage and zealous labors of a political party, ...but he should strive to be always mindful of the fact that he serves his party best who serves the country best.

Rutherford B. Hayes

A Place in Time   Stan St. Clair

Fictional Characters:

William Graham "Will" Patterson
William Patterson Senior
William Graham "Billy" Patterson II
Mary Lou Graham Patterson
Other Graham family members
Little Emma
Colonel Walker
Jane Walker
Sally Walker Patterson
Tom Walker
George Walker
Other Walker family members
Hal Bright
Mammy Flora
John Price
Sam Long
Patty Duke
Billie Jean Smith
Bessie Jackson
Joe Jackson
Nashville Doctor

Epilogue:
Jane Patterson
William Graham Patterson III
Sara Patterson

A Place in Time   Stan St. Clair

Historical Characters

President Abraham Lincoln
President Andrew Johnson
Eliza McCardle Johnson
President Ulysses S. Grant
President Rutherford B. Hayes
President Thomas Jefferson
President James A. Garfield
Nancy Hanks Lincoln
Abraham Enloe
Wesley Enloe (picture)
Tom Lincoln
Thomas Lewis
John McHenry
Booker T. Washington
General Irvin McDowell
General Ambrose Burnside
General Stonewall Jackson
Senator Thaddeus Stevens
Senator Benjamin Butler
Senator Hiram Rhodes Revels
Senator Jefferson Davis (picture)
Captain Charles S. Schaeffer
General George Armstrong Custer
Tenn. Governor,
"Parson" William G. Brownlow
Secretary of War Edwin Stanton
Senator Edmond G. Ross

A Place in Time   Stan St. Clair

Congressman William Lawrence
Senator Charles Sumner
Dred Scott
Congressman Thomas Jenckes
Congressman Robert Ridgway
Congressman Alexander Rives
Congressman Richard T. W. Duke
Attorney General Amos T. Akerman
Attorney General Alfonzo Taft
Judge George Logan
General William Tecumseh Sherman
Miss. Governor Adelbert Ames
Samuel Tilden

Epilogue:
Dr. Martin Luther King
President Barack Obama

www.ingramcontent.com/pod-product-compliance
Lightning Source LLC
Chambersburg PA
CBHW031403040426
42444CB00005B/404